REMARKABLE CANADIANS

Avril Lavigne

by Galadriel Watson

Published by Weigl Educational Publishers Limited
6325 – 10 Street SE
Calgary, Alberta, Canada
T2H 2Z9

Website: www.weigl.com

Library and Archives Canada Cataloguing in Publication

Watson, Galadriel
     Avril Lavigne / Galadriel Watson.

(Remarkable Canadians)
Includes index.
ISBN 978-1-55388-307-4 (bound)
ISBN 978-1-55388-308-1 (pbk.)

     1. Lavigne, Avril--Juvenile literature. 2. Singers--Canada--Biography--
Juvenile literature. I. Title. II. Series.

ML3930.L412W33 2007   j782.42166'092   C2006-906245-5

Printed in the United States of America
1 2 3 4 5 6 7 8 9 0 11 10 09 08 07

Editor: Liz Brown
Design: Terry Paulhus

We acknowledge the financial support of the Government of Canada through the Book
Publishing Industry Development Program (BPIDP) for our publishing activities.

Cover: Avril Lavigne has won many music awards in her career.

Photograph Credits
Courtesy of Janine Murray, page 6; Registered by the Government of Ontario under the
Trade Marks Act: page 7 top left.

Every reasonable effort has been made to trace ownership and to obtain permission
to reprint copyright material. The publishers would be pleased to have any
errors or omissions brought to their attention so that they may be corrected
in subsequent printings.

Contents

Who Is Avril Lavigne?

Avril Lavigne is a musician. She sings and writes songs. In 2002, Avril released her first album, *Let Go*. She was 17 years old. Two years later, Avril released her second album, *Under My Skin*. Both were great hits. On these CDs, Avril sings about subjects like boys, skateboarding, and her hometown. **Fans** love her catchy **rock and roll** tunes and great fashion sense. They also love her outgoing personality.

> *"I'm gonna dress what's me, I'm gonna act what's me, and I'm gonna sing what's me."*

Growing Up

Avril Ramona Lavigne was born in Belleville, Ontario, on September 27, 1984. She has an older brother named Matt and a younger sister named Michelle. Her mother, Judy, works at home. Her father, John, works as a telephone **technician**.

When Avril was five, her family moved to the farming town of Napanee, Ontario. In Napanee, many people play sports and listen to country music. Avril listened to country music. She played hockey with her brother in a boys' hockey league. She played baseball and was a good pitcher. When Avril was in grade 10, she discovered skateboarding. As a middle child, Avril always tried to stand out. She dreamed of being a rock star.

🍁 Before Avril became well known, she attended Napanee District Secondary School. A picture of Avril now hangs in the hall of the school. This is in recognition of her achievements in music.

Ontario Tidbits

COAT OF ARMS

MINERAL
Amethyst

FLOWER
White Trillium

Toronto is the provincial capital of Ontario.

The Great Lakes are located in Ontario.

Ontario was one of the first four provinces to join **Confederation**.

Toronto is the largest city in the province.

More than 11 million people live in Ontario.

Think about it!

Avril grew up in a small town in Ontario. She lived far away from any major city. How do you think living in a **rural** community affected her music?

Practice Makes Perfect

When Avril was two years old, she began to sing at church. By age 10, Avril was singing a **solo** in her church Christmas **pageant**.

Soon after, Avril would pretend her bed was a stage. She would stand on it and sing. She would imagine that she was surrounded by adoring fans. Avril always planned on being a well-known musician. She knew that she would have to work hard to be successful. Avril practised often and worked hard.

Even though Avril is a successful singer, she still has to practise before her concerts.

When Avril was 11 years old, she began teaching herself how to play her father's guitar. She started writing her own songs.

Avril began performing at local fairs and talent shows when she was in high school. Her parents bought her a sound machine so that she had background music for her shows.

🍁 Now that Avril is well known, she travels around the world to give performances in stadiums and record stores.

When Avril was 14, she won a radio contest. As a prize, she was asked to sing with Shania Twain, a well-known country singer, during one of her concerts. Avril eagerly accepted.

A year later, a man heard Avril sing in a bookstore. He was impressed by her talent, and he became her **manager**. He booked her for many performances. At age 16, Avril travelled to New York City to work with a group of music writers and producers to improve her singing and writing skills. While she was there, she met a **music producer** who worked for Arista Records. He gave her a **contract** to make her first album.

In 2002, the album was released. It was called *Let Go*. This album was extremely popular and sold 14 million copies worldwide. Avril spent most of her time touring and giving concerts to make people more interested in her album.

In 2002, Avril performed at the MTV Video Music Awards in New York City.

Thoughts from Avril

Avril always planned on being a rock star. Here are some things she has said about her life.

Avril has always had a strong personality.

"To understand me you have to meet me and be around me. And then, only if I'm in a good mood..."

Avril travels to New York.

"I just got there and I was like, 'Ok, I have work to do.'"

Avril writes songs for _Under My Skin_ with musician Chantal Kreviazuk.

"We got together one night and all of a sudden we had a song."

Avril's CD _Let Go_ is a success.

"I have this awesome opportunity to fulfill my dream."

Avril performs with Shania Twain.

"It was the biggest rush of my life...I was the happiest person in the world."

Growing up, Avril liked playing sports on boys' teams.

"I was always a **tomboy** and I guess I still am."

What Is a Musician?

A musician is a person who makes music. Musicians can sing or play instruments. Avril sings and plays the guitar.

Many musicians do not make much money from their music. They have other jobs and make music just for fun. Others, such as Avril, are professional musicians. This means that they make money from performing and recording their music. These musicians spend their time writing and recording songs, selling CDs, and performing in front of audiences.

Many musicians practise at home in their basement or garage.

Musicians 101

Shania Twain (1965–)

Type of Music: Country
Achievements: Twain is one of Canada's best-known country singers and **songwriters.** Her first album was released in 1993. Twain's third album, Come on Over, has sold more copies than any other album by a female solo artist. More than 34 million copies have been sold. Twain has won 12 Juno Awards. These awards recognize the achievements of Canadian musicians.

Bryan Adams (1959–)

Type of Music: Rock and Roll
Achievements: Adams was one of Canada's top-selling rock and roll musicians in the 1980s. Since 1980, he has released 16 albums. One of his most popular albums, Reckless, sold about seven million copies. His other albums have also been successful. Adams has won 18 Juno Awards.

Nelly Furtado (1978–)

Type of Music: Urban
Achievements: Furtado released her first CD, Whoa Nelly, in 2000. Since then, Furtado has won 10 Juno Awards. Her third CD, called Loose, was number one on the Billboard Album sales chart in June 2006. Furtado also hosted the 2007 Juno Awards, which were held in Saskatoon, Saskatchewan.

Michael Bublé (1975–)

Type of Music: Jazz
Achievements: Bublé has won five Juno Awards and three Canadian Smooth Jazz Awards. The Canadian Smooth Jazz Awards recognize accomplishments in jazz music. Bublé's album, It's Time, was the bestselling album in Canada by a Canadian artist in 2005. It has sold more than four million copies around the world.

Guitars

Many musicians play the guitar. An acoustic guitar makes sound when the player plucks one of the guitar's six strings. The vibrations move about inside the hollow guitar and get louder. An electric guitar sends the vibrations to an **amplifier** and speaker.

Influences

Many people influenced Avril's career in music. Her mom and dad supported her interest in music. Avril's father played music. It was his guitar that Avril first learned to play. When Avril was 11 years old, her parents bought her a guitar.

Growing up in a small town, Avril had many opportunities to practise her skills. At night, she would keep her family awake while she practised playing the guitar and singing in front of the mirror. Avril's parents encouraged her to sing. Avril's mother called her a "little songbird."

Avril listened to country and church music. She especially loved country artists, such as Shania Twain, Faith Hill, the Dixie Chicks, and Garth Brooks. Avril liked the way that these artists sang country music. They used rock and roll sounds in their songs.

Avril is still close with her family. In 2004, she took her brother and sister to the MuchMusic Video Awards in Toronto.

Avril's older brother had an album by a band called the Goo Goo Dolls. Avril enjoyed listening to the album. Then, she learned about other bands, such as Third Eye Blind, and Matchbox 20. Avril realized that she did not want to perform country music. Instead, she wanted to perform rock and roll.

When Avril was given the chance to record her first CD, her parents agreed to let her travel to New York City. They sent her older brother along to keep her company. Even when Avril is busy promoting her music and touring, her parents try their best to keep in touch with her.

GARTH BROOKS

Country musician Garth Brooks was an important influence on Avril. He first became well known in 1989. Although he sang country music, Garth added rock and roll to his songs. This made country music more popular than it had been before. Many young people, such as Avril, began listening to country music.

Garth Brooks has won two Grammy awards during his career.

Overcoming Obstacles

Even though Avril has done well, she has faced many challenges. Before Avril became well-known, her manager sometimes had a difficult time booking her for performances. This was because many of the places where live bands played only allowed adults to perform. Avril was too young.

Even when Avril was given a contract to record an album in New York City, there were difficulties. The record company thought Avril would sing country music. In the past, that was the type of music she had performed. Avril wanted to sing rock and roll. The record company sent songwriters to help Avril create her songs. However, she did not want to sing the songs they wrote.

Many people who travel to New York City visit the Statue of Liberty. It is located on Liberty Island.

After spending four months in New York City, Avril decided to move to Los Angeles. The record company had her work with a new set of songwriters. With their help, Avril created the songs on *Let Go*.

For *Under My Skin*, Avril wanted the music to represent her personality. She did not know what she was going to write, so she sat down with her friend Chantal Kreviazuk. Together, they wrote songs that speak of more personal feelings.

When Avril released *Under My Skin*, she sang at many malls around the United States and Canada. She called this her "Top Secret Mall Tour."

Achievements and Successes

Avril has achieved great things for someone so young. Less than six months after *Let Go* was released, the album had sold nearly 14 million copies worldwide. *Let Go* had many number one songs. *Under My Skin* was also a bestselling album with several hit songs such as "My Happy Ending" and "Don't Tell Me."

The first award Avril won was in 2002. It was an MTV Video Music Award for her song, "Complicated." This is when Avril first felt she had achieved success. In 2003, Avril received four Juno Awards. These included awards for best new artist and best album. She won three more Juno Awards in 2005. Avril was also nominated for eight Grammy awards. The Grammys recognize special achievements in music.

Avril has many fans around the world. She has performed in cities such as Toronto, New York, and Berlin.

Avril has appeared in many magazines. In 2006, for example, *People Magazine* named her one of the "Most Beautiful People in the World." Avril also has begun acting. In 2006, she was the voice of Heather the opossum in the children's movie, *Over the Hedge*. She had small parts in the movies *Fast Food Nation* and *The Flock*.

In April, 2007, Avril released her third album. The first single from the album was called "Girlfriend." It **debuted** on the Billboard Hot 100 chart at number five. This was the best debut of Avril's career.

AVRIL'S CHARITY

Avril supports several charities, or organizations that help people, and urges her fans to do the same. She has sung on **benefit CDs** for Amnesty International, War Child, and and the U.S. Campaign for Burma. These organizations help protect people. She has performed at concerts to raise money for victims of the **tsunami** in Asia and **SARS** victims in Toronto. She has appeared in ads that help the fight against AIDS.

In 2002, Avril sang and signed autographs for fans at a concert in New York City, to raise money for public schools.

Write a Biography

A person's life story can be the subject of a book. This kind of book is called a biography. Biographies describe the lives of remarkable people, such as those who have achieved great success or have done important things to help others. These people may be alive today, or they may have lived many years ago. Reading a biography can help you learn more about a remarkable person.

At school, you might be asked to write a biography. First, decide whom you want to write about. You can choose a musician, such as Avril Lavigne, or any other person you find interesting. Then, find out if your library has any books about this person. Learn as much as you can about him or her. Write down the key events in this person's life. What was this person's childhood like? What has he or she accomplished? What are his or her goals? What makes this person special or unusual?

A concept web is a useful research tool. Read the questions in the following concept web. Answer the questions in your notebook. Your answers will help you write your biography.

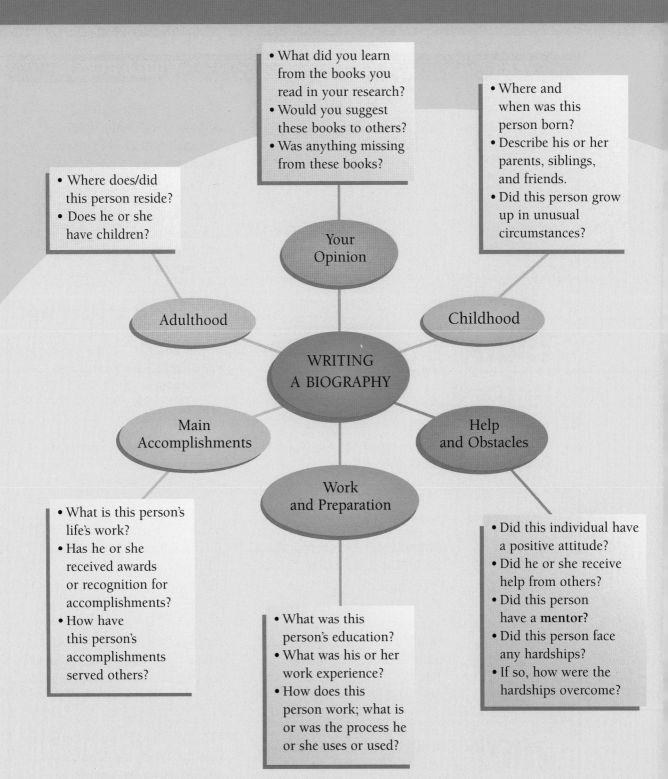

- What did you learn from the books you read in your research?
- Would you suggest these books to others?
- Was anything missing from these books?

- Where and when was this person born?
- Describe his or her parents, siblings, and friends.
- Did this person grow up in unusual circumstances?

- Where does/did this person reside?
- Does he or she have children?

Your Opinion

Adulthood

Childhood

WRITING A BIOGRAPHY

Main Accomplishments

Help and Obstacles

Work and Preparation

- What is this person's life's work?
- Has he or she received awards or recognition for accomplishments?
- How have this person's accomplishments served others?

- What was this person's education?
- What was his or her work experience?
- How does this person work; what is or was the process he or she uses or used?

- Did this individual have a positive attitude?
- Did he or she receive help from others?
- Did this person have a **mentor?**
- Did this person face any hardships?
- If so, how were the hardships overcome?

Timeline

YEAR	AVRIL LAVIGNE	WORLD EVENTS
1984	Avril Ramona Lavigne is born on September 27.	MuchMusic is launched on August 31 in Toronto. It is Canada's first 24-hour music television station.
1994	Avril sings a solo at her church's Christmas pageant.	Green Day release their album, *Dookie*, on February 1. This album influences many **punk** bands in the 1990s and 2000s.
1999	Avril wins a radio contest and is invited to sing with Shania Twain at a concert in Ottawa.	Britney Spears releases her debut album, *Baby One More Time*, on January 12. By the end of the year, the album had sold ten million copies.
2002	Avril releases her album, *Let Go*, on June 4, 2002.	U2 performs at the Superbowl halftime show.
2004	Avril releases her second album, *Under My Skin*, on May 25, 2004.	Usher releases his album, *Confessions*, in 2004. It sells 1.1 million copies during its first week in stores.
2006	Avril marries Sum 41 singer and guitarist Deryck Whibley on July 15.	Red Hot Chili Peppers have the best-selling new-release album of the year with *Stadium Arcadium*.
2007	Avril releases her third album on April 16, 2007.	The Dixie Chicks win album of the year for *Taking the Long Way* at the 2007 Grammy Awards.

Further Research

How can I find out more about Avril Lavigne?

Most libraries have computers that connect to a database for researching information. If you input a key word, you will be provided with a list of books in the library that contain information on that topic. Non-fiction books are arranged numerically, using their call number. Fiction books are organized alphabetically by the author's last name.

Websites

To learn more about Avril, visit her official website at www.avrillavigne.com

To learn about the Juno awards and Juno award winners, visit www.junoawards.ca

Words to Know

amplifier: a type of electronic equipment that makes sounds louder

benefit CDs: albums made to raise money for charity

Confederation: the creation of Canada in 1867

contract: a written agreement to do something

debuted: made a first appearance

fans: the people who listen to a musician's albums and go to concerts

manager: the person who controls a musician's business

mentor: a wise and trusted teacher

music producer: the person who arranges for an album to be made

pageant: a type of play or musical

punk: a type of rock music that celebrates rebellion and anger

rock and roll: a popular type of music that started in the 1950s

rural: in the country

SARS: severe acute respiratory syndrome, a type of illness

single: a song sent out for radio stations to play

solo: a performance that is done alone

songwriters: people who write songs for a living

technician: a person who looks after and repairs technical equipment

tomboy: a girl who likes to dress and act like a boy

tsunami: a huge ocean wave caused by an earthquake

Index